LINKEDIN

The Sandler Way

*25 Secrets That Show Salespeople
How to Leverage the World's Largest
Professional Network*

Sandler Training

Linked in Sales Solutions

Paperback: 978-0-692-45394-0
E-book: 978-0-692-44605-8

Special Thanks

Any book worth reading is a collaborative effort, this one more than most. The list of helping hands here is a long one, but one name in particular stands out from all the rest. Special thanks go out to Koka Sexton for his support and guidance and for his many invaluable contributions to this project.

CONTENTS

PART 1: CHANGE THE GAME

PART 2: CREATE A CLIENT-FOCUSED, CLIENT-ATTRACTING PROFILE

PART 3: GET CONNECTED

PART 4: SEARCH FOR QUALITY PROSPECTS

PART 5: MAKE CONTACT

PART 1

Change the Game

Make it simple to connect with
prospects using LinkedIn

CHAPTER 1

You're Not Alone

Social selling is not as tough as it seems

Sandler Training began work on this book because we've found that many sales professionals struggle with this mysterious task called "social selling." It's the kind of thing they know they should do—the kind of thing they are often told they're doing incorrectly—and maybe they even get frustrated with themselves because they sometimes don't know what to do.

The good news is that social selling is easier and more intuitive than most people think. The 25 "secrets" (including this one) contained here are only secret in the sense that, for most salespeople, the topics uncover best practices that haven't yet become part of a sales team's daily culture. The key is to use, share, and reinforce these ideas. Our first request to you, then, is that you be willing not only to learn, but to adopt and model these best practices so that they become the practical daily realities of your selling day, not only for yourself, but for everyone in your organization who sells for a living.

Don't forget, too, that you have help if you need it. Feel free to visit www.sandler.com to connect with a Sandler® trainer who will keep you up-to-date on all the newest social selling information.

CHAPTER 2

Social Selling for Anyone Who Sells for a Living

Put LinkedIn Sales Navigator to work

F ull disclosure: Sandler is a ceaseless, dedicated advocate of LinkedIn and its Sales Navigator application. Whether or not you're currently using Sales Navigator, we thought you might be interested in our answers to the most common question we get about this resource. Professional salespeople from various industries say to us: "My time is tight. With all the other resources for salespeople out there that I could invest my time figuring out, why is Sales Navigator worth the learning curve?"

SHORT ANSWER #1: THE LEARNING CURVE IS RIDICULOUSLY SHORT

The time-to-mastery gap for Sales Navigator is very short—you will be up and running in under a day. The guiding force driving this tool is this question: "Why not make it simple for sales-people to connect with prospects via LinkedIn?"

It's easy to get started, learn best practices and achieve success with this tool. This video gives you an overview: bit.ly/sales_navigator.

SHORT ANSWER #2: IT'S SIMPLER THAN WHAT YOU'RE PROBABLY DOING NOW TO GENERATE LEADS

Sales Navigator gives you an easier, more intuitive way to view more prospects. It will almost certainly make it easier to leverage your own network of contacts and those of your company than what you're doing now. It allows you to access the networks of people within your own organization in a way you aren't able to with free LinkedIn or any other platform.

That means if Jim in Accounting is connected to Juan, a prospective buyer you want to meet, it will be easier for you to figure that out and far simpler to connect to Juan than the way you're selling now.

BY THE NUMBERS

On average, social-selling leaders
enjoy these benefits:

- *45% more opportunities created*
- *51% more likely to achieve quota*
- *80% more productive*

(Source: LinkedIn Sales Solutions)

LinkedIn Sales Navigator helps sales professionals
be more successful at social selling by leveraging
300M+ professional profiles and 2M+ company pages.

SHORT ANSWER #3: IT PUTS YOU IN CONTROL OF A PROVEN SOCIAL-SELLING PROCESS

Sales professionals are increasingly finding value in building their own leads and pipeline through social selling. Sales Navigator is designed to quickly get you to the point where you use social selling intuitively, every day, to identify and engage with live prospects who connect to your LinkedIn network.

When we talk to Sales Navigator users about why the tool is of value to them, what we hear is that it answers a question that's been left unanswered. There has been a lot of discussion in recent years around the question, "What is social selling?"—but the right answer has sometimes been hard to formulate. Sales professionals wanted to master social selling, but they found there was no agreement on exactly what it was and no way to operationalize it consistently across an entire sales team. There wasn't one tool that made social selling a viable daily reality for everyone on the team. The question became: Wouldn't life be a lot easier if there were?

LinkedIn Sales Navigator is the manifestation of that vision. It makes social selling easy and available to everybody.

You don't have to be a LinkedIn wizard, and you don't have to know how to do advanced searches or find a dozen different ways to work your way through the system to get things done. You can use your own network of business contacts and your company's network to take an account-centric view of the world. This tool cuts through all the noise.

SHORT ANSWER #4: YOU DON'T HAVE TO CHANGE ANYTHING YOU'VE ALREADY SET UP

Sales Navigator integrates seamlessly with your CRM tool and makes it more powerful. You can sync up the data daily.

For a free 30-day trial of LinkedIn Sales Navigator, please visit: bit.ly/sales_navigator.

PART 2

Create a Client-Focused, Client-Attracting Profile

Use your LinkedIn profile to appeal to a specific target audience

CHAPTER 3

Supercharge Your LinkedIn Profile

Set a solid foundation for your social selling

L et's face it, most LinkedIn profiles don't make very interesting reading.

For salespeople, that's a problem. Consider: A LinkedIn profile is a perpetual introduction to the online world. That profile is up and running 24 hours a day, 7 days a week. It's often the first or second thing that comes up when someone searches for a person's name. In short, it's an opportunity.

But if your LinkedIn profile bores people, makes them think you're trying to pressure them into doing something they don't feel like doing or leaves them wondering what you're trying to say, you're in trouble. If you don't fix the problem, you are mishandling your virtual introduction to countless potential customers, every minute of every day. Any salesperson who consistently botches the introduction is likely to encounter some career problems!

BY THE NUMBERS

There are an average of 53 million views of LinkedIn profiles each day.

(Source: LinkedIn Sales Solutions)

The main thing for salespeople to remember about LinkedIn is this: It is a huge, never-ending, virtual networking event—and you always have to be ready with the best response to the question, "What do you do?"

That's the question your LinkedIn profile is supposed to answer. But most salespeople write their profile as though they were being asked other questions. For instance: "What is your career history?" Or: "What is your company's history?" Or: "Can you please describe all the features of your product/service?"

Sandler trainers teach salespeople how to create a powerful, high-impact, 30-Second Commercial they can use to answer the question "What do you do?" or any of its variations in a way that piques a prospective customer's interest and creates a larger, mutually beneficial business discussion. The approach we use works in all industries. If you build your own effective 30-second commercial and incorporate it into your LinkedIn profile, you will dramatically improve your profile's effectiveness as a marketing and sales tool.

"WHAT DO YOU DO?"

To create a good 30-second commercial, consider the "What do you do?" question from the point of view of a prospect in pain who eventually turned into your happy customer. Then start writing—and rewriting.

For instance, you might write: "We specialize in custom-designed inventory management systems for manufacturing and distribution operations. We've been particularly successful with companies in the X, Y and Z industries that are concerned about the costs associated with inaccurate inventory counts, unhappy with frequent paperwork bottlenecks that slow down the fulfillment process or disappointed by the amount of time it takes to reconcile purchasing, invoicing and shipping records. We've been able to create hand-in-glove inventory management systems that help our customers save time, attention and money."

SALES ACCELERATOR

A good 30-second commercial uses hot-button words that connect directly to human emotion: "concerned," "unhappy" and "disappointed." These are the sentiments a prospect in pain experiences.

Notice that the commercial above focuses only on problems that a specific type of prospect would recognize. There are no company/personal histories or feature dumps. Also notice that, true to its name, the 30-second commercial doesn't go on forever!

If something like this isn't on your LinkedIn profile, you're at a competitive disadvantage.

BY THE NUMBERS

Your LinkedIn profile should answer the perennial question: "Is what this person does relevant to me?" It should specify a particular industry. Members who have an industry listed on their profile receive, on average, 15 times more profile views than those who don't.

(Source: LinkedIn Sales Solutions)

CHAPTER 4

3 LinkedIn Profile "No-Brainers"

Enhance your visibility and your
impact with likely buyers

t's surprising how many salespeople overlook these 3 simple
steps for optimizing their LinkedIn profile. Take a look. How
many have you completed?

NO-BRAINER #1: COMPLETE YOUR LINKEDIN
PROFILE TO 90%+ AND KEEP IT CURRENT

The first step toward improving your social selling is making
sure your LinkedIn profile facilitates sales rather than inhibits
them. Below are the essentials for having a complete profile.

BY THE NUMBERS

50% of B2B buyers say they won't work with sales professionals who have an incomplete profile.

(Source: LinkedIn Sales Solutions)

Profile picture: Adding a picture makes your profile 7 times more likely to be viewed by others, so make sure you have one that shows you at your professional best.

Custom URL: LinkedIn assigns a generic URL to your profile, but a custom URL looks more professional. In addition, adding your custom URL to your email signature will increase the likelihood of others engaging with you on LinkedIn.

LINKEDIN LESSON

You can customize your public profile URL when you edit your public profile. Custom public profile URLs are available on a first-come, first-served basis.

1. *Move your cursor over "Profile" at the top of your homepage and select "Edit Profile."*
2. *Click the URL link under your profile photo. It will be an address like "www.linkedin.com/in/yourname."*
3. *Under the public profile URL section on the right, click the "Edit" icon next to your URL.*
4. *Type the last part of your new custom URL in the text box.*
5. *Click "Save."*

Summary: This is where you can share your skills and expertise and create a compelling story of how you can provide value to your prospects. If you are in sales, your summary should speak to your ideal buyer.

After making sure everything is current, try scheduling a monthly or quarterly reminder to analyze your profile for additional upgrade opportunities. Whether it's gaining a recommendation from an esteemed colleague or adding a certification or accomplishment, keep adding recent credits and accomplishments. No prospect has ever looked at a profile and said, "Whoa, this sales rep is a little too credible and trustworthy."

BY THE NUMBERS

Listing your education details on your LinkedIn profile makes you 10 times more likely to draw profile views than people who don't.

(Source: LinkedIn Sales Solutions)

NO-BRAINER #2: ADD AT LEAST ONE MULTIMEDIA PRESENTATION

An effective way to grab your prospect's attention is by adding multimedia content to your profile. Pertinent links, videos, SlideShare presentations and white papers go a step beyond simply telling your prospects what you can do to actually showcasing your value. Your marketing department can be a good source of this content if you have not created any yourself. Start out by adding one piece of multimedia content this month. Revisit it throughout the year, adding new content whenever you think it will provide value to your clients and prospects.

NO-BRAINER #3: EASY ON THE "I"

You may be tempted to spend most of your profile text talking about yourself. That's a mistake. The goal of your profile must be to catch and hold the attention and interest of a specific group of people: your target market. That means it can't be all about you!

Too many LinkedIn profiles make it look like the salesperson is looking to get hired. The work history section of your profile shouldn't read like a resume. Update it to be a more personal description of what you accomplished at each of your jobs and connect each of those accomplishments to a specific pain or problem that is typically experienced by your ideal prospect.

IN A NUTSHELL

Your profile should say, not "Here's how wonderful I am," but "Here's the outcome we help people like you accomplish." Remember, the star of the show is not you, nor your company history, nor the features of your product/service. It's the result you deliver consistently to your happy customers.

Make sure your profile is focused narrowly on the real-world business problems of your chosen market. Paint a mental picture for the reader of the outcome that you can provide that resolves those problems.

Build out the summary section of your profile by including things that are of value to the people who are going to read your profile, even if what you find seemingly has nothing to do with your company. Find the best articles related to your industry, pick one and put that article into your profile, so that it becomes a resource.

THE TRUSTED ADVISOR

These three simple steps—completing your LinkedIn profile, adding a multimedia presentation and de-emphasizing the "I" factor—will allow you to showcase yourself as a credible, trusted advisor with whom it is easy to work. Here's the best part: Your LinkedIn profile is always working for you—whether you are logged on or not!

CHAPTER 5

Make Sure Your LinkedIn Profile Calls the Prospect to Action

Invite your reader to reach out to you via LinkedIn in your summary

The first section of your LinkedIn profile that people see is the summary. It should come right out and say that you are open to conversations with people who could benefit from a professional relationship with you, and it should say how to start that conversation.

The kind of "call to action" language we're talking about— simple but routinely overlooked by salespeople—might read like this:

Connect with me on LinkedIn if you want to talk about (X)
[where X is the problem you solve or the value you add].

That's the first, and most important, call to action you should build into your profile. If possible, include your email and telephone information.

BY THE NUMBERS

Many summaries on LinkedIn are too short! You have plenty of room to include a strong call to action in your summary. A summary of more than 40 words dramatically increases your likelihood of turning up in a LinkedIn search.

(Source: LinkedIn Sales Solutions)

OTHER CALLS TO ACTION

In addition to your summary's invitation to connect, you should consider building other calls to action into your profile, both direct and indirect. A direct call to action could be an invitation to request a special report of direct interest to your target audiences. An indirect call to action might be a link to some kind of rich media that directs to a landing page that captures information about your prospect.

Whatever "freemium" you offer as a call to action, it should be linked directly to the problem you solve and the value you and your organization add by solving that problem.

BY THE NUMBERS

Unless your target audience is exclusively domestic, avoid "calls to action" that mention specific countries, currencies or localities. Your LinkedIn profile is accessible to over 300 million professionals in over 200 countries and territories.

(Source: LinkedIn Sales Solutions)

MAKE THE CALL TO ACTION CRYSTAL-CLEAR

People need to know the next steps in your purchase process, and your LinkedIn profile should offer at least one such next step. Make it simple. Make it impossible to miss. Make it easy to take.

If you don't give people a clear call to action, they won't know what to do with the information, insights or intelligence you have provided or hinted at in your profile. The call to action

IN A NUTSHELL

Make sure there is a clear step-by-step process in place for people whose interest you've aroused with your profile. It might sound like this: "To get our free white paper on the three most common mistakes people make when handling X challenge, click here."

should give them a chance to find out a little more about what working with you would be like.

If potential clients are in any way confused about what to do after seeing your message, they will decide to look elsewhere for answers—probably your competition's website.

CHAPTER 6

Harness the Power of Third-Party Endorsements

Make sure your profile provides social proof that you and your organization can deliver

Social proof can take many forms and can be delivered through any number of channels. The social proof that shows up on your LinkedIn profile should point toward at least one recent downloadable case study and should be supported by recent endorsements and recommendations from your network of LinkedIn contacts.

One thing a lot of salespeople are afraid to do is go back to the customer after the fact and ask for a recommendation. Sales

> ## SOCIAL PROOF
>
> *A recent article in* Forbes *magazine defines "social proof" as "a psychological phenomenon where people assume the actions of others reflect correct behavior for a given situation."*

professionals should be doing this systematically. It's important to know who your best customers are, and you should be willing to ask them, specifically, for recommendations on LinkedIn.

Social proof on LinkedIn is not a "nice to have." It's a "must have." What you say about your product, service or company—the claims you make—are not likely to be that different from what your competitors are saying about their product, service or company. It's the social proof verifying what you say—the recommendations, endorsements and case studies you get from those who have used your service, have been satisfied with it and are willing to tell why—that adds value to your message.

> ## POTENT QUOTE
>
> *"It is not uncommon for someone to tell me after viewing my LinkedIn profile and reading the recommendations, that this is a deciding factor on whether or not to contact me and/or use my services."*
>
> —LinkedIn user quoted in *Forbes* magazine, May 14, 2014

IN A NUTSHELL

When you say you can do something, a prospect might take that with a grain of salt. But when 10 other people for whom you've done a good job step forward and say, "Yes, not only has he done it, but he's done it more quickly, and less expensively, than we expected," that adds value and credence to your message and gives prospective buyers a reason to take another step with you.

When a prospect who is looking to buy something comes across your profile and sees that lots of different people who work at lots of different companies all have something nice to say about you, that opens up trust. It adds professionalism and credibility to your profile. Your profile is not complete unless it has this kind of social proof.

HOW MUCH SHOULD YOU HELP?

Sometimes salespeople ask whether it's OK to craft the actual language of a recommendation for them on LinkedIn. It's not.

If you have to craft the final wording of the recommendation, it's not truly genuine. With that said, it's common for some people to say to a salesperson, "I would love to give you a recommendation, but I'm a horrible writer. Can you give me an idea of what you're looking for?" In these cases, it's all right

BY THE NUMBERS

You are 12 times more likely to be viewed for potential opportunities if you have more than one position listed on your profile.

(Source: LinkedIn Sales Solutions)

to give the person a list of possible bullet points or to show the person the kinds of recommendations other clients have provided.

That kind of help can start the process, but the final language needs to be your client's, not yours.

CHAPTER 7

Play Straight

Don't game the system—it makes
your profile look amateur

There are people out there who type the word "process management" and then copy and paste it into their LinkedIn profile 50 times or so. It looks absolutely ridiculous, and it doesn't work.

If your profile looks like all you are trying to do is play the system, what kind of message are you sending to the world? Are you showing that you are a professional person committed to integrity, communicating clearly and delivering solid value? Not with those kinds of games.

KEEP IT REAL

Of course, if it makes sense to mention the term "process management" in your profile, and if you end up doing that five or six times without looking like you're trying to fool a piece of software, that's a different story. If you can find creative ways to build a certain word or phrase into your profile unobtrusively while staying authentic and maintaining the message of professionalism that you're sending out to the world, it's not a problem.

Your aim is to come across as (and be) someone who can be trusted—not someone who's out to pull a fast one. The same basic principle applies to all your interactions on LinkedIn, but it's particularly important to remember as you put together and regularly update your profile.

From a personal and professional branding standpoint, if you want to be found under "excellent leadership," or "management," or any other category, your best bet is not to repeat the phrase as many times as possible. Take advantage of the work others in your organization have already done. Find the latest material your marketing department has put together around that key phrase, and then build their content into your profile.

IN A NUTSHELL

*Don't repeat words or phrases in
your profile robotically.*

OTHER EXAMPLES OF "GAMING THE SYSTEM" TO AVOID

Unfortunately, keyword stuffing isn't the only example of game-playing to be found in LinkedIn profiles. You should also avoid:

- **Fake or ghostwritten recommendations.** LinkedIn is all about relationships with real people you know. Don't pretend to know people you don't. Avoid putting words in people's mouths.

- **Exaggerated or misleading career information.** Don't say you have experience you don't. This will always backfire—it's only a question of when.

- **Mentioning high-profile contacts who have no idea who you are.** If someone would be surprised to see you mentioning him in your profile, don't do it.

- **Passing along links you haven't actually used or visited.** Only include verifiable, authentic links in your profile that actually add value for your target prospect.

CHAPTER 8

Company Pages 101

Post a snapshot of the pain your company removes

Your company page will reap major benefits if you work with your marketing colleagues to create a powerful 30-second commercial for your company as a whole. (As opposed to a 30-second commercial for a single salesperson.) This is a very brief capsule summary of your product/service offering that tells prospective buyers about a pain or problem that is familiar to them—and how your company alleviates that pain.

Notice that a good 30-second commercial is not a recitation of your company's history, or its founder, or the names of its products and services. Here, for instance, is a 30-second commercial that doesn't work:

Logistical Planning Associates is a full-service software application development firm founded in 1982 by Guy You Never Heard Of. We are located in Anywhere, USA, with satellite offices in Littletown, Midburg and Large City, USA. Our company motto is "Quality, Value and Service." We specialize in inventory management, and we have over 100 qualified programming professionals who are focused like a laser beam on living up to that motto of ours. To learn more about what we do and how we do it, click here.

Snore. How much of that is focused on the prospect? Two little words buried in the middle: "inventory management."

A good 30-second commercial that focuses on the prospect, by contrast, can lay the foundation for a compelling LinkedIn company page. Take a look at this example.

Logistical Planning Associates specializes in custom-designed inventory management systems for manufacturing and distribution operations. We've been particularly successful with companies in the X, Y and Z industries that are concerned about the costs associated with inaccurate inventory counts, unhappy with frequent paperwork bottlenecks that slow down the fulfillment process or disappointed by the amount of time it takes to reconcile purchasing, invoicing and shipping records. We've been able to create hand-in-glove inventory management systems that help our customers save time, attention and money. We'd love to talk to you about your inventory management issues: click here to connect with us.

THE PLAN

If your company is going to build a strategic sales plan around its LinkedIn page (and we certainly hope it is), management should ensure that all employees are following the company page.

Here's why. When you become a follower of a page, your entire network knows. That means if a dozen or a hundred salespeople follow the company page, there are going to be tens of thousands of people who see that the company page exists. That's good for business.

CONNECT WITH THE TEAM

Use the same kind of employee activation to drive awareness of your company. For instance, all of a company's sales professionals should be encouraged to share news from the LinkedIn company page with their network. They can do that by adding commentary, by "liking" the article or through any number of other social actions. When that kind of sharing happens and a salesperson engages on the platform about company-generated content, their whole network sees the engagement and that the news is spreading.

This is one of those places where an overlap with sales and marketing happens. The marketing people need to push updates onto the company page on a regular basis, but also they need to ensure that those updates are not going to be perceived as too self-promotional. The news the salespeople share has to add value to their customer base.

If you've been personally tasked with the job of setting up your company's LinkedIn page, be sure to check with your marketing people or the senior people in your company so they can sign off on what you've done. Make sure what you're planning on posting is in sync with the rest of the company's messaging.

IN A NUTSHELL

Just as your profile shouldn't be too "me-focused," the company page shouldn't be too "company-focused." Place your spotlight on the value your company delivers in dealing with the common challenges and problems of your customer base.

PART 3

Get Connected

Use LinkedIn to create and expand a
powerful, self-updating contact list

CHAPTER 9

Use the News Stream to Generate More Leads

The news stream generates new leads and nurtures existing sales opportunities

I f you are an account executive, your company depends on you for consistent sales lead generation. Generating qualified leads means uncovering new opportunities. It also means nurturing your "not quite ready to buy" prospects so that you gain access to the buying cycle once they transition from consideration to evaluation.

Question: How do you do that on LinkedIn?

Answer: You use Sales Navigator.

CREATING SAVED LEADS

The first step in setting up your news stream is to create a list of saved leads. You can import data from your CRM to receiving automatic updates on key accounts and prospects. LinkedIn Sales Navigator also makes lead recommendations, uncovering potential industry targets based on data inputs for whom you are targeting.

Once you have a list of saved leads, you will be alerted to company news and status updates of your contacts, such as job changes and work anniversaries. Additionally, you'll learn when prospects publish blog posts, join LinkedIn groups and share content. Feed settings allow you to pick the specific updates you'd like to receive.

MONITOR BUYING SIGNALS

Daily updates from your saved leads can signal where your prospects are in their buying process. For example, prospects often engage in LinkedIn groups to find answers to pressing questions or to ask about specific vendor solutions. When you see prospects engaging in this manner, you can feel confident of their intent to buy.

Get an additional indication of prospect intent from company updates and news mentions in your news stream. For example, news of an acquisition or geographical expansion may trigger an additional need for the solution you offer. Find the trigger events that create demand for your solution and monitor them closely.

Staying on top of personnel changes at your target accounts can improve your sales lead generation results as well. Newly hired decision makers tend to make their mark early, which is why executives who move into new positions usually make major purchases in their first year on the job.

ENGAGE WITH INSIGHTS

Once you have identified a buying signal, use insights to engage your prospects. For instance, you can engage prospects who ask questions in LinkedIn groups by sharing insights from your company's content.

When armed with the right insights, news regarding your prospect's company is also actionable. When key accounts make the news (and when there's a relevant tie-in to your solution), try crafting a thoughtful InMail to your prospect that connects

IN A NUTSHELL

For account executives with an opportunistic mindset and a helpful attitude, the news stream is filled with lead-generation opportunities. Dedicating a few minutes each day to examining your news stream for new opportunities to engage prospects with insights can help you build stronger relationships and uncover more qualified leads, which naturally generates better sales numbers.

the dots between the current event and the potential business problem(s) you can solve.

FEEL FOR WARM PATHS TO PROSPECTS

The LinkedIn Sales Navigator news stream can help to secure warm introductions by alerting you to when prospects in your saved leads connect with someone in your network.

Knowing someone in common can build trust with a prospect so that a buyer is more receptive to outreach. The effect can be especially powerful when you use the system to get introduced to a prospect. A prospect is far more likely to engage through your shared connection than through cold outreach.

BY THE NUMBERS

Of B2B buyers, 69% are more likely to buy from a vendor recommended to them than a vendor who isn't.

(Source: LinkedIn Sales Solutions)

Taking a strategic approach to news stream updates can help you turn insights into actions, all without committing a great deal of time to prospecting. In the process, you can establish yourself as a trusted authority on whom B2B decision makers can rely.

For a free 30-day trial of LinkedIn Sales Navigator, please visit: bit.ly/sales_navigator.

CHAPTER 10

Use This Checklist to Respond Quickly without Sacrificing Quality

Just a few minutes can make the difference between winning and losing a sale

eacting quickly matters in the world of sales lead generation. If you doubt that, read the text box!

> ### BY THE NUMBERS
>
> *A recent study from Lead Response Management revealed that a prospect is 100 times more likely to respond when a seller reaches out within 5 minutes as opposed to reaching out 30 minutes later.*

What does that mean? It means that when you get word via LinkedIn that someone is interested in talking to you about what you and your company have to offer, you have just minutes, not hours, to respond. How do you prepare a meaningful message within such a short timeframe? To help you quickly qualify prospects so you can form a fast yet intelligent response, here is a checklist of items to review on LinkedIn.

FIRST, CHECK PROSPECT'S PROFILE

The prospect's company, title and objectives are found at the top of his LinkedIn profile. This information can help you craft the start of your response by addressing the person appropriately.

Go further down the page to learn about your prospect's role within the company and search for valuable information such as business goals, challenges and accomplishments. Anything that helps you understand his needs (both individual and corporate) will allow you to better reach out with solutions that meet those needs.

SALES ACCELERATOR

Can't view the prospect's profile because he is outside your network? With the team edition of LinkedIn Sales Navigator, you are able to unlock 25 profiles per month of people beyond your third-degree connections.

SECOND, CHECK SHARED CONNECTIONS

Decision makers are 5 times more likely to engage with you if the outreach is through a mutual connection. If you have shared connections with your prospect, mentioning them in your outreach—with permission, of course—can help you capture attention. Using the "get introduced" feature can be especially effective in establishing instant trust. If you can, share a resource you know to be of value to this shared contact.

When sharing strategic content with prospects, be sure to explain how it can help your prospect accomplish a known business goal. By demonstrating your knowledge and leading with insights in a timely manner, you'll have a distinct advantage over your competition.

IN A NUTSHELL

Leverage your network by using the "how you're connected" feature on the right side of user profiles. When appropriate, engage with common connections to learn more about your prospect or request an introduction.

THIRD, CHECK RECENT ACTIVITY

Your prospect's recent activity on LinkedIn may reveal important insights. Has he recently added new connections, joined a group, liked content or followed a page? Any of these activities may allow you to learn what your prospect currently finds useful and relevant.

The LinkedIn groups your prospect belongs to may reveal his business objectives and where he is in the buying cycle. Discussion comments can provide insights on prospect needs, pain points and problems the person is looking to solve. This knowledge can be used to craft your response and demonstrate how you can provide value. Participating in LinkedIn groups can also help you discover new prospects in a helpful, professional context.

Remember to follow the Golden Rule when interacting with prospective buyers in LinkedIn groups: Do unto the prospect as you would have done to you! When you post a question or engage in a discussion, you prefer helpful answers and meaningful conversation, not a sales pitch. This is exactly what your prospects want and expect as well.

Move more leads into the "live opportunity" stage by striking while the iron is hot. Use the three-part checklist above to craft a quick, thoughtful response.

CHAPTER 11

Strike the Right Connection Balance on LinkedIn

Adopt a value-based connection philosophy

E veryone who uses LinkedIn has a connection philosophy, though some people would probably have a hard time describing their philosophy in words. Maybe you're one of those people who aren't sure what your connection philosophy is. Since you sell for a living, we want to suggest that you make a conscious choice to adopt a connection philosophy that supports both you and your organization.

There are three dominant connection philosophies that Sandler has seen on LinkedIn. Most people fall into only one of these three categories. The problem is, only one of these philosophies—the third one—works best for professional salespeople. We are hoping you will choose to adopt that philosophy for yourself.

PHILOSOPHY #1: THE OPEN NETWORKER

People who adopt this philosophy look at LinkedIn contacts a little like dedicated baseball fans look at baseball cards—the more you can get, the better. You can't have too many!

These people are pretty easy to notice because they amass a whole lot of contacts. If they were to put their connection philosophy into words, it might sound like this: "I am an open networker. I will connect with anyone and everyone under the sun. My goal is to have 50,000 connections on LinkedIn." Many of these folks view their total number of LinkedIn connections as a kind of status symbol, a marker of their social standing.

PHILOSOPHY #2: THE CLOSED NETWORKER

People who adopt this philosophy look at handing out LinkedIn contacts about the same way they look at handing out hundred-dollar bills. You don't give them to just anyone!

The philosophy of the closed networker sounds something like this: "I'm not going to connect with you on LinkedIn unless I sit down with you, order a good meal at a nice restaurant, shake your hand and decide that I like you." You've probably run across your share of people on LinkedIn who have adopted this philosophy.

PHILOSOPHY #3: THE VALUE NETWORKER

We think sales professionals need to find the middle ground between these two extremes. It doesn't need to be dead center, of course, but it should be somewhere in the middle. Salespeople need to be able to articulate why they occupy that middle ground.

The middle position that works most often for salespeople is based on a very simple question: "Can I, as a sales professional, add value to you?" If the answer to that question is "Yes," you should probably add that person as a contact. You may or may not get a lot of value from this person, at least right away, but if you're certain that you could conceivably add value to this person's world with what you and your company offer, you're going to be open to the possibility of adding him as a contact. Of course, you should add people from whom you know you will learn or receive other kinds of value.

IN A NUTSHELL

A value-based connection philosophy drives the most successful sales professionals on LinkedIn.

Whatever you decide to share on LinkedIn should ultimately relate to the value you deliver to your clients and customers. It should not be about what a great person you are, what your kids are up to, what new piece of trivia you found or what funny video you just saw. LinkedIn is focused on business. Stay focused on what you provide for the people who keep your company afloat—your customers—and try to find more people like them. Work from the context of their expectations and the outcomes they want. That's why you're on this platform.

CHAPTER 12

You Are Not the Company Page

Don't try to be the face of the organization

Consider this: Each time you add someone to your network with whom you are unlikely to exchange actual value, the following things happen:

Pros

- You can market to a wider audience.
- You can search and see more people in your network.
- You will feel more important and influential.
- You can improve your brand recognition and rankings.

Cons

- You water down your networking, as you see a lot more unwanted junk in your news feed.

- It will be harder to follow up and keep track of relationships.
- You can lose credibility with your referral partners if you don't know people with whom they want to connect, or you connect with someone they don't like or respect.
- The platform becomes less valuable because you lose a personal connection to people and organizations with whom you want to interact.

The best practice when it comes to taking advantage of both sides of this argument—which is what a lot of people tell us they want to do—is to create a LinkedIn company page to represent the "face of the organization." Here you can market to a wide audience; at the same time, you can keep your individual profile limited to close connections. Of course, you should follow your own organization's company page.

Mike Montague, a Sandler trainer, recently wrote on this topic. Mike points out: "On LinkedIn, your company page can be followed by anyone and you don't have to add anyone back (though of course you can). Alternatively, lots of organizations will have a CEO, owner or president who serves as the face of the organization, and that company leader can add as many people as he wants. Using either kind of page, you expand the marketing reach and support the marketing and public-relations goals, and the salespeople in the organization can keep their personal networks tight and maximize the sales benefits."

That's good advice. You should also consider using LinkedIn Sales Navigator's TeamLink function to expand your reach to your entire sales team's LinkedIn connections. TeamLink is, to put it bluntly, a game-changer.

For a free 30-day trial of LinkedIn Sales Navigator, please visit: bit.ly/sales_navigator.

CHAPTER 13

Stay on the Right Side of 500

Keep your personal network tight

I f you're a salesperson with more than 500 LinkedIn contacts, here's an interesting question for you. How many of those people could you call and be absolutely certain that the individual in question would either take your call or return it within 24 hours?

Most salespeople with over 500 LinkedIn contacts tell us that, for the majority of those contacts, they would have to say more than their name and company in order to keep the person from ducking or rejecting the call.

Is that really what most of your network should look like?

More than 500 LinkedIn connections may sound like a great idea for salespeople, but if many of your contacts are inactive or even hostile, there comes a point where the numbers don't help. It may be time to consider disengaging from contacts who don't pass the "phone test."

Of course, if you are getting started or have less than 150 connections, you can approach this question very differently. In that situation, you should consider taking advantage of LinkedIn's suggested connections for you. This is a great place to start.

LinkedIn can gauge how much you have in common with someone and how likely you are to know that person. These lists typically go on forever, so don't feel you need to sort through all of them. The most likely candidates for good connections show up at the top, and you can check back in at any time.

Another good way to build your network is to download the LinkedIn app and sync your phone connections. Not only will this import your phone contacts to LinkedIn so you can connect with them, but it also allows you to download your LinkedIn connections to your phone. In many cases, this will give you additional contact information.

Beyond that, you should think about your real-life network. Whom do you know, like and trust, and who knows, likes and trusts you? All those people should be in your network.

You probably have good relationships with vendors, investors, coworkers, clients, association and other networking partners. You might also know industry influencers, referral partners and government or media contacts. I also recommend reaching out to complementary businesses. Think about who knows the people you want to know. Who calls on the same prospects as you, either before or after they need your services?

When in doubt, connect with people who are likely to want to talk to you about what you do. Remember, in social selling, your goal is to build relationships, not an audience. Too many contacts can actually make it difficult to start conversations because your network will be clogged with people for whom you can't really add value.

CHAPTER 14

Invest Your Time in Building Social Capital

Bring value to your LinkedIn network

The only proven way to build social selling skills is to build relationships and create social capital. Of course, LinkedIn is a great place to do that. It allows you to become a strategic advisor and trusted consultant for your network. We'd like to challenge you to think about how you can bring the greatest amount of value to your personal network of LinkedIn connections.

Maybe you have expertise your connections don't have, maybe you can listen and solve problems or maybe you have a unique perspective or background on a subject of interest to them. There are lots of ways you can bring value to your network.

In Bob Berg's great book *The Go-Giver*, he points out that, contrary to popular belief, it is not the go-getters who achieve the most success—it's the go-givers. The ones who make the most deposits in their network end up making the most deposits in their bank account.

The go-getters run around frantically trying to grab their piece of the pie, while the go-givers realize that by helping other people get what they want, they will build the relationships and social capital to get what they want. This is true of the most successful businesspeople on the planet.

SALES ACCELERATOR

In his essay "Compensation," Ralph Waldo Emerson says that each person is compensated in a manner consistent with the way in which he has contributed. That principle is proven every day on the LinkedIn platform.

Some people think that giving to others is a sacrifice. However, David Sandler, the founder of our company, pointed out that it is not a sacrifice to trade something of lesser value for something of greater value. That's called an investment. There is actually a quantifiable return on giving. By giving more, you get more.

What are some specific ways you can give to your social network? Here's a list to get you started:

- You can give (reality-based) testimonials and recommendations to others.
- You can share your expertise and write helpful articles.
- You can be a curator of great ideas and share others' expertise.
- You can make introductions for other people to help them get or give help.
- You can like and share things that people in your network will care about and post.
- You can invest your time in them, take them to lunch or even just listen.
- You can form strategic alliances by sharing someone's most helpful piece of information with your network.
- You can answer questions, give feedback and share an article specific to someone's unique challenges.
- You can cultivate a LinkedIn group for people with a specific interest or facing a specific challenge.

The possibilities really are endless, if you're looking at the relationship with a giving attitude.

There is one caveat. You must remember that the bottom line of all this activity is going to the bank. While you're doing all this giving, you have to constantly keep your antenna up for a sales opportunity.

Luck, as the saying goes, is preparation meeting opportunity. While you are preparing your networking and building relationships, you still have to recognize opportunity and take advantage of it. If you run into a prospect who is ready to buy or who mentions a problem that you know you can solve, don't wait. That is the time to transition your relationship-building into a selling opportunity.

CHAPTER 15

5 Traits of Today's B2B Buyer

Learn the common traits that extend
across buyers in all industries

I t's impossible to create one profile that describes every B2B
buyer. Organizational needs vary greatly by industry, and buyers approach the decision-making process with unique priorities. There are 5 characteristics, however, that describe most B2B
buyers in the social-selling era. Learn about these prominent
qualities and discover how you can leverage your network to
reach today's buyers.

1. B2B BUYERS ARE MORE TECHNOLOGY-RELIANT THAN EVER

Professionals are often too busy to meet in person. Phone calls are regarded as disruptive, not productive. Computers, tablets and smartphones rule the day.

Research shows that much of the B2B buying process has gone online. More specifically, it's gone social.

2. B2B BUYERS CAN CHOOSE FROM A WIDE RANGE OF PRODUCTS, SERVICES AND PROVIDERS

B2B professionals can find many vendors online, making it critical for brands to capture prospects' attention early in the buying cycle. An effective way for sales professionals to engage early-stage prospects is through warm-path outreach.

Research shows that 69% of B2B buyers are more likely to choose a vendor who has been recommended to them, so rely on your network to identify connections who can help you initiate relationships with second- and third-degree connections.

BY THE NUMBERS

A 2014 IDC study revealed that 3 out of 4 B2B buyers and 8 out of 10 executive buyers rely on social media to help make buying decisions.

3. B2B BUYERS CAN COMPLETE ALL OR MOST OF THE DECISION-MAKING PROCESS WITHOUT YOU

Today's buyers complete roughly two-thirds of the buying process on their own, without input from sales professionals. You can still be influential early in the buying process, but that often requires being proactive and quick on your feet.

One strategy is to save contacts and organize them with tags. By saving contacts, you can monitor your LinkedIn feed daily for buying signals that can help identify new sales opportunities.

4. B2B BUYERS ARE LOOKING FOR VALUE-ADDED PARTNERSHIPS WITH SOLUTIONS PROVIDERS

Given that today's B2B buyers can navigate most of the purchasing process on their own, they tend to selectively choose consultative partners who provide the most value during the buying journey.

Sales professionals must be ready to listen to buyers' needs and provide individualized solutions that respond to unique challenges and priorities. Leading your outreach with customer-centric insights shows you are serious about understanding the customer and providing value.

5. B2B BUYERS HAVE HIGHER EXPECTATIONS FOR SALES REPS AND SOLUTIONS PROVIDERS

More choices allow buyers to be choosier. They can dictate the terms of how they do business and with whom they do it. That means you must effectively articulate your value proposition to win sales.

As B2B buyers seize more control of the decision-making process, the most successful sales professionals will be those

SALES ACCELERATOR

One way to differentiate yourself from other providers is to demonstrate thought leadership in your industry. You can do this by:

- *Highlighting achievements, recommendations and professional affiliations in your profile.*
- *Sharing and commenting on insightful articles in your areas of expertise.*
- *Answering questions and participating in discussions in LinkedIn groups.*
- *Producing content that addresses vital industry topics or common buyer questions on the LinkedIn publisher platform.*

Getting recognition as a thought leader requires a long-term commitment to providing your network with information of value. While casting yourself as a trusted authority takes time and effort, it can yield a big payoff: 90% of B2B buyers are more likely to engage with sales professionals seen as thought leaders.

who use a helpful, consultative approach that emphasizes value. How can you adapt your sales methodology to cater to new buyer trends?

CHAPTER 16

4 Best Practices for LinkedIn Groups

Master these 4 simple strategies for success

In a different world than the one we sell in now, you would hold nothing but in-person meetings with prospects who wanted to talk to you about challenges you could help them to overcome.

You'd be absolutely certain that the prospect was serious about the business relationship because the person took time out of a busy day to meet with you, one-on-one, with both of you right there in the same room. You'd be able to monitor all the body language and vocal tonality firsthand. You'd never have to wonder whether the prospect was paying attention or not. You'd know by looking and listening. The telephone would hardly ever ring to interrupt your meeting, and there would be no such thing as social media to distract your prospect, either. You'd shake hands—literally, not virtually—at the end of each meeting, ideally having scheduled the next face-to-face meeting.

But that's not the real world—not anymore.

In today's world, physical interactions with prospects are few and far between. Anytime you can have a face-to-face meeting, of course, that is the best scenario. But the reality is that you can reach exponentially more people by getting involved in the right LinkedIn groups.

If you are presenting yourself in a positive manner in your profile; if you are giving value to that group; if you are asking the right questions; if you master the special etiquette of online interaction (which is different than that of an in-person meeting)—then that group will generate plenty of good discussions with prospective buyers.

Unlike an in-person conversation, effective participation in a LinkedIn group will pass along prospecting dividends for years to come. Ponder that. Let's say you're going to a networking event today and you meet 20 people. You may have a powerful positive impact on five of them, but that's about it. Anything else that comes of those discussions will be a result of your follow up.

But when you go into a LinkedIn group and add value with a suggestion or ask a great question, that contribution will stay there forever. If people search for that topic, your interaction is going to appear. You'll be associated with it for years after you hit "post."

It's definitely worth taking a few moments to learn and practice these 4 simple principles of effective LinkedIn group dynamics for salespeople.

BY THE NUMBERS

Salespeople are 70% more likely to get an appointment with a prospect if they reference a mutual LinkedIn group during outreach.

(Source: LinkedIn Sales Solutions)

PRINCIPLE #1: ONLY JOIN GROUPS THAT MATCH YOUR BUSINESS FOCUS

Prospects can see what groups you join. Make sure they can get a good picture of what your specialty is just by glancing at the list.

PRINCIPLE #2: MIND YOUR MANNERS

Of course, you'll avoid any unprofessional or inappropriate behavior here, but there's more to it than that. Different groups have different standards, and it is likely to take a little while for you to figure out what the vibe is in any given community. Once you've joined a group, spend some time noticing how its most respected members contribute and how often. Then, follow their example.

PRINCIPLE #3: REMEMBER—NO HARD SELL

The whole point of taking part in the group is to pose questions that forward the conversation and share information that adds value. You don't want to fall into the trap of offering free consulting, yet you are there to share insights and expertise when people ask for help. That's the opposite of a hard sell. It's a balancing act: knowing how much of your expertise to give away in a discussion and how much to withhold. Sandler's advice is to give LinkedIn group members a tasty "hors d'oeuvre" of knowledge when doing so helps at least one member of the group who has asked for it. Make sure you've received a purchase commitment, though, outside of the group, before you serve the whole meal.

PRINCIPLE #4: CONSIDER CREATING AND MANAGING A LINKEDIN GROUP OF YOUR OWN FOCUSED ON A PROBLEM OR CHALLENGE YOUR IDEAL PROSPECT FACES

While starting a group of your own is a long-term commitment, it can yield immense dividends. It boosts your credibility, makes people want to connect with you and (eventually) generates great off-line discussions about what you and your company offer. The only way this can go off-track is if you forget Principle #3 above.

CHAPTER 17

How Often Should Salespeople Post on LinkedIn?

Identify the right frequency for you

L ots of salespeople ask us: "How often should I post on LinkedIn? And what, exactly, should I be posting?"

There are probably as many "right" answers to these questions as there are salespeople. But some broad principles can help you find the right answer for your situation and your market.

"HOW OFTEN SHOULD I POST?"

Some people manage to post more or less on the hour, throughout the business day, but for most salespeople that's not ideal. Sandler's advice is to look at how many posts you're currently publishing and at the engagement level you're generating. If everything you post elicits a relatively high level of engagement (a few likes and a couple comments per post), you could probably be posting more. On the other hand, if you're posting so much that people can't keep up, you're doing too much.

Lacking any other benchmarks, your minimum for the day should probably be three or four posts. That may sound like a lot at first, but it's really not. Post a couple of items first thing in the morning, another one after lunch and one more thing during what we call your "you hour"—the time when you decompress at the end of the day and transition out of work mode.

We talk to lots of salespeople who say they post regularly but don't see any positive results. This is usually either a situation where the person is posting at or less than once a day or is posting material that doesn't add much value.

LINKEDIN LESSON

You can share thoughts, articles or other content-rich websites from your homepage and several other places. This is sometimes known as "sharing an update." Use the share box to post a wide variety of information:

- *From your homepage*
- *From discussions in your LinkedIn groups*
- *From partner sites like the* Wall Street Journal *or the* New York Times
- *From LinkedIn* Pulse
- *From any webpage when using the LinkedIn sharing bookmarklet*
- *To re-share a member's update or a company page update with your own comments*
- *To re-share a member's update or a company page update with no change to original content*

"WHAT SHOULD I POST?"

This is a big question. How you update your network determines how the world will perceive you and your company. Don't take that decision lightly. Put some time and effort into choosing what you share with your network.

As a general but reliable rule, you should be posting a variety of content: information about your industry, resources your customers and prospects can use or updates from your marketing department about your company. Switch it up and keep it interesting. Don't get too buttoned up—let your personality show. Use a quote, image or infographic that speaks to your chosen audience. Break it up so your feed is not just a bunch of random text updates.

SALES ACCELERATOR

You don't need a huge amount of graphic design talent, a whole lot of money or even much time to come up with an infographic that brings your LinkedIn feed to life and engages your network. Here are 3 free resources you can use to create a killer infographic:

- *piktochart.com*
- *easel.ly*
- *developers.google.com/chart*

You can also make powerful images, charts and visual quotes in PowerPoint and then save them as pictures to upload to LinkedIn.

IN A NUTSHELL

Use your posts to distribute specialized knowledge of direct interest to targeted prospects—but only enough to make them want to reach out to you for a discussion.

CHAPTER 18

3 Tactics to Strengthen Relationships with Prospects

Move the discussion forward

Social selling is a lot like dating. Once you've made that initial connection, the challenge is to figure out how to go from first-date-worthy to relationship material.

To help you use social selling to become "the one" to your prospect, we combed through research on interpersonal and social relationships to uncover 3 scientifically-proven tactics you can use to strengthen relationships with your sales prospects:

1. RESPOND IN AN ACTIVE-CONSTRUCTIVE WAY

When prospects share good news on LinkedIn, they are subtly signaling that they want to connect. To develop your relationship, "turn toward" a prospect by leaving an active-constructive comment. Research has shown that when a person responds to a request for connection with supportive words and questions, the recipient feels closer to the person and more satisfied with the relationship. Neutral responses, such as "That's great!" have a much smaller impact.

When a prospect posts good news, respond in one of two ways:

1. **Confirm the importance of the news and elaborate on positive implications.** "The research you just published is excellent. Looks like you'll be in the running." "Congrats on the promotion! Does this mean that you'll be managing a bigger team?"
2. **Reinforce your relationship by revealing knowledge about the personal significance of the news.** "Congrats on the promotion. Looks like all those early mornings paid off!"

2. REACH OUT IN NEW WAYS

There is a lot of debate over the best communication channels for establishing a relationship with a prospect. Should you send an InMail, leave a comment or engage in a discussion in a LinkedIn group?

The answer is that you should use all of the channels offered by LinkedIn to reach out to prospects. Studies show that people form stronger relationships when they use multiple means of communication. Research also shows it is possible to strengthen ties by adding an additional means of communication.

To build a strong bond with prospects, use as many relevant communication tools as possible. If you see a prospect share an article in your LinkedIn feed, leave a comment, then send an InMail that expands on your response. Reply to discussions in LinkedIn groups, and make sure you like and share interesting content posted by your prospect. The more channels you use to reach out to prospects, the more connected they will feel to you.

3. BECOME A STORYTELLER

When researchers at the University of Utah studied the Bushmen of Africa's Kalahari Desert, they found that stories told by campfire at night had a bigger impact on relationships than the "how to" conversations held during the day. Stories cement ties between the storyteller and listener and build a sense of community.

To sound like a storyteller when you reach out to prospects, answer the following questions when you leave a comment, engage in a discussion or send an InMail:

- Who is the hero of this story?
- What is the hero trying to accomplish?
- What obstacle gets in the way of achieving this goal?
- Who or what helps the hero achieve the goal?
- What is the moral of the story? What does the hero learn?

Enhance your bond even further by using a persona or industry-specific stories. The more prospects can relate to the hero of your story, the more understood they will feel.

Build your relationships on LinkedIn by responding in an active-constructive manner to good news, communicating through multiple channels and telling stories when you engage with prospects. These tactics will allow you to form a deeper bond in less time and create the quality relationships that turn into long-lasting, revenue-producing accounts.

PART 4

Search for Quality Prospects

Use LinkedIn to generate warm referrals
from your existing contact network

CHAPTER 19

3 Do's and 3 Don'ts for Prospecting in the Social Selling Era

Use LinkedIn daily to move the right relationships forward at the right time

The explosion of social media has created lots of new opportunities for your company when it comes to sales prospecting. Utilizing the tools available to you can, in the best-case scenario, expand your business and deliver a source of continuous lead generation—or, in the worst case, cause an embarrassing publicity nightmare. Here are 3 best practices to bear in mind, followed by 3 worst practices to avoid, as you leverage your presence in business-related social media channels.

#1: DO CONNECT, INFORM AND ENGAGE

Social media posts are not a replacement for active outreach, but they can and should support your prospecting campaign. For that to happen, everything you post in business settings (like LinkedIn) should have the three-part goal of connecting with a specific type of person, informing the person of something relevant and previously unknown and engaging in a way that helps you find out whether your product/service is a good fit for that person. These three things, in the best case, happen almost simultaneously in social media channels, which is why they are consolidated here.

#2: DO LET THE DATA WORK FOR YOU

Use social media for data mining. Social media sites such as Facebook and LinkedIn are great tools for lead generation, but many salespeople overlook the reality that these sites can give valuable insights into customer demographics. Today's environment is fraught with oversharing, and sales professionals can use that to their advantage. There are filters available for many social media sites that can sort your audience by age, gender and other categories. This lets you focus more closely on your clients and target customers more specifically. In particular, LinkedIn's Sales Navigator application brings data acquisition and prospect targeting to a whole new level. Sales Navigator can sync daily with your CRM.

#3: DO RESEARCH THE COMPETITION

It's amazing how few salespeople use social media platforms to learn about their competition's weaknesses. This is perhaps the best way to gain critical insights on how to improve your own customer experience. Many, many customers take to Facebook, Twitter and LinkedIn to provide feedback on their user experience. Translation: Customers complain there, hoping someone will notice. If you are not looking at your competitor's social media stream on a regular basis, you are missing out on learning about their weaknesses. Once you have an understanding of those shortcomings, you'll be able to highlight your strengths and meet needs the competitors can't. (Of course, you'll want to listen just as closely to your own customers' feedback.) By the way, this "Do" also gives you another way of prospecting to an already targeted customer. If someone is unhappy due to a bad experience with your competitor, see #1 above. Connect, inform and engage!

#1: DON'T ASSUME EVERYONE IS A PROSPECT

No matter how big your network is or how many friends you have on Facebook, it's guaranteed that most of them are not qualified prospects for your product or service. That only makes sense, right? So take that to its logical conclusion. If people don't need your services (and most of them won't), they aren't going to want to hear or read a 10-minute pitch on why your product or service is great. Don't waste your time.

#2: DON'T MIX BUSINESS AND SOCIALIZING

This "Don't" is particularly relevant to discussions on LinkedIn. Remember: This social network is all about business. Discussions about your kid's graduation pictures, the latest celebrity scandal or that funny cat video just don't belong.

#3: DON'T GET SO BUSY YOU GO BROKE

In the online age, it's easier than ever for salespeople to imagine they're being productive when they're not. There's always the danger of "constructive avoidance"—busywork that keeps you from reaching out to people and having real-time business conversations about whether or not it makes sense to work together. Come to LinkedIn with a clear purpose: identifying qualified prospects. A qualified prospect is one who has a pain you can alleviate, who can commit to a budget and who will share his organization's decision-making process with you with complete transparency. Use LinkedIn to generate more real-time conversations about these issues, not avoid them. Sometimes salespeople tell us, "I'm doing research—I'm trying to identify my ideal prospect." OK, but if that takes two and a half hours for each prospect, you've got a problem. Some activities drive and support the selling process, and some don't. It's your job as a professional salesperson to know which is which.

CHAPTER 20

Target Smart

Meet TeamLink

With Sales Navigator, LinkedIn now allows you to focus on your target accounts with more potential points of contact and more information than ever before, leveraging all kinds of information on new and existing relationships. Specifically, that means you can:

- Discover new leads with recommendations tailored to you.
- See existing relationships within the company.
- See everyone you've saved at the account and easily access their profiles.

- Use TeamLink to find colleagues who are connected via LinkedIn to people at the target account.

That last point is worth examining closely. It changes everything.

BY THE NUMBERS

Typically, only 6% of salespeople are connected, via LinkedIn, to everyone in their own company. TeamLink challenges that.

(Source: LinkedIn Sales Solutions)

Usually when you are searching for a decision maker and trying to figure out how to leverage a connection to reach that person, you're working blind. You don't have enough resources available to you. Now you can leverage TeamLink—a functionality that will allow you to leverage your whole company's LinkedIn contact networks.

TeamLink allows you to target smart. You are exposed to tens of thousands of connections. If you are looking for a certain VP of Whatever and you don't have connections leading directly to that person, you may find that, thanks to TeamLink, you have connections to his boss or someone who reports directly to him.

TeamLink is a game changer. It's one of those tools that a lot of companies have tried to build but couldn't because they don't have an effective LinkedIn profile. With TeamLink, you'll be able to leverage your entire company's social graph and find the connections you need to make these introductions. Time and again, companies leveraging TeamLink report that their sales are exploding.

BY THE NUMBERS

A major financial services company recently increased its pipeline by 4,000% by leveraging its LinkedIn connections via TeamLink.

(Source: LinkedIn Sales Solutions)

TeamLink gives sales teams a huge competitive advantage. Now they have a way to operationalize social selling so the entire sales team gets the most out of the organization's cumulative LinkedIn connections. It's a breakthrough idea. If you want, it's yours for a month, as part of the Sales Navigator package. For a free 30-day trial of LinkedIn Sales Navigator, please visit: bit.ly/sales_navigator.

CHAPTER 21

The Stress-Free LinkedIn Referral

Leverage the strongest initial connection, the one made through an introduction and endorsement

LinkedIn is a great networking resource, but most salespeople haven't mastered the art of using it to generate referrals. Here's one technique that's worked for John Rosso, one of Sandler's franchisees. John writes:

> Let's assume you, Bill Jones, are one of my first-degree LinkedIn contacts, and I see that you're directly connected to David Smith, to whom I want to be connected as well. What do I do? I send you an email or InMail message, a message that says something like the following:

Hey there, Bill, I happened to notice on your LinkedIn profile that you're connected to David Smith over at Acme Corporation. How well do you know him? Would you be willing to introduce me?

Typically, you will reply with something like this:

Sure. I know David very well. He and I went to college together. I'd be happy to introduce you.

My return email to your message will say:

Bill, I got your message. I really appreciate that. My experience is that an email introduction can work very well for everybody involved. I have attached a template for your review. Please feel free to edit and change it in any way you want.

The template I attach will look like this:

David, this is John. I wanted to take the opportunity to introduce the two of you. David is a good friend of mine, and John is a sales training specialist who is engaged with a number of my clients and who does top-notch work. John, I would ask that you reach out to Dave and set up a time to speak. If either of you want me to be part of that conversation or have any questions, please reach out. All the best, Bill

Assuming you approve of my proposed message, or something like it, you will then send the message out to me and to Dave. Then I will send an email in response:

> Hey, Bill, thanks so much for the introduction. Dave, I'm really looking forward to speaking with you. I'm out of the office on Monday, Tuesday and Wednesday of this week, but I will be back in on Thursday. I will reach out to you by phone then. What's the best number to use to reach you?

I've just set up a phone appointment!

Remember the whole principle that makes networking on LinkedIn work is having some kind of actual person-to-person communication with your first-degree contacts. If I've never had any interaction at all with you before I reach out to you about Dave Smith, the technique I've just outlined won't work. Don't try to extend this kind of appeal to someone with whom you really have no contact.

(Of course, if you know Bill well, you can always pick up the phone and call for the introduction. That's up to you.).

IN A NUTSHELL

Use LinkedIn to generate referrals in a way that leaves everyone feeling OK.

PART 5

Make Contact

Use LinkedIn to support a solid
prospecting and selling plan

CHAPTER 22

The 9 Commandments of Social Selling

Memorize and follow them all!

H ere are 9 social selling tips that can make it easier for sales prospects to want to do business with you.

1. PROVIDE A SOLUTION THAT DOESN'T INVOLVE BUYING ANYTHING

It's easy for sales professionals to help prospects solve a problem when the solution is to buy something. They get rid of a pain point, and you get a sale. It's a no-brainer—for you. If you really want to show them how much you care, put your expertise to work on a problem that doesn't have a sales so-lution. It's the difference between doing the dishes with the hope that your spouse will fold the laundry, and doing the dishes because you know your spouse is happier when the dishes are done.

2. BE MINDFUL OF THEIR TIME WHEN SHARING CONTENT

When sharing helpful content with prospects, show that you respect their time by making it easier to gain value from the content. Take the extra step to curate relevant details from white-papers and e-books. If you're sharing content from YouTube, you can pause, right-click and select "Get the Video URL at the current time" to generate a link that starts playing at a specified starting point.

BY THE NUMBERS

Videos on landing pages increase conversions by 86%.

(Source: Social Fresh)

3. SEND A DETAILED AGENDA IN ADVANCE OF YOUR MEETING

Many prospects skip sales meetings because they're not entirely sure what's in it for them. A detailed agenda shows you've considered the meeting from their point of view. You already know what you're presenting and that it will be of value; make sure they do, too.

4. MAKE YOUR DEMOS SPECIFIC TO THE PROSPECT'S PROBLEMS

If you've taken time to research the specific problems you can solve for your prospect—and let's hope you have—carry this knowledge into your demo. Structure your demo around the prospect's needs and say, "I know you have X problem, and this feature of the product will do Y to solve it." A buyer-centric demo is more useful and less boring for the buyer, which means it's more likely to elicit a favorable response.

5. LEAD WITH INSIGHTS

If you come across a dynamite article that speaks to something your prospects care about, take the time to forward it to them. Bonus brownie points for adding a comment along the lines of, "I understand you've been interested in X. Here's a post I came across that made me think of you." If you struggle with finding content, a few minutes each day searching LinkedIn *Pulse* or other industry news sites can have a big impact.

6. MAKE YOUR PROSPECT LOOK GOOD

If you've been following your prospects on LinkedIn, you likely have developed a sense of their goals and motivations. If you can help them further their career goals, they'll be more likely to help you with yours. You can also volunteer to write a recommendation of the skills they've demonstrated in your professional relationship. Just make sure you take the time and effort to write the kind of recommendation you'd want to receive.

7. MAKE THEM FEEL UNDERSTOOD

As in romantic relationships, sometimes the best thing you can say to prospects is nothing at all. Take the time to listen to what they hope to gain from a purchase or what specific hurdles they're facing. Showing some genuine empathy can go much further than demonstrating the perfect sales solution, especially at the outset of your relationship.

8. SHARE THEIR CONTENT OR UPDATES WITHOUT PRESSURE TO RECIPROCATE

When your prospects write status updates or long-form posts on LinkedIn's publishing platform, they're trying to make their voice heard. You can respond by leaving an insightful comment or simply sharing their content with your network. Show that your motive is to be helpful by not immediately following up with a request for a sales meeting. Relationship building is easier when your actions aren't always tied to your own agenda.

9. PLAY MATCHMAKER

This is one of the few situations when you can show love for someone by introducing him to someone else. Use the broad professional network you've built to spot people who aren't connected yet but could mutually benefit from being introduced. When you broker this type of introduction, you've added value for two people simultaneously.

Just like your significant other, your prospects don't really need fancy gifts. What they need is to know that you respect their time and value them as partners. When you go out of your way to add value to the relationship, you show that you're in it for more than a sale. It takes a little time, but it's worth the effort—and it'll save you a fortune on flowers and chocolate.

CHAPTER 23

Avoid These 5 LinkedIn Worst Practices

Avoid these prospect alienators
and deal-killers at all costs

K eep in mind, sometimes just sharing best practices isn't
enough. Below, a list of 5 deadly sins we've seen more than
one salesperson succumb to on LinkedIn. We won't name
names, but we will insist that you don't follow their example.

#1. PRETENDING TO KNOW SOMEONE YOU DON'T

Sooner or later, it blows up in your face. If you say, "I'm connected with Joe on LinkedIn, and I think you and I should chat,"

that had better not come as an unpleasant surprise to Joe. If you know the person would not return your call, don't pretend he is your number one cheerleader.

#2. FAILING TO PROOFREAD YOUR PROFILE

If you can't spot basic grammar and spelling errors, enlist the aid of someone who can. Ideally, everyone on the sales team should read everyone else's profile. That way, you're all catching mistakes and spreading best practices.

#3. NOT MAINTAINING A PROFESSIONAL STANDARD OF BEHAVIOR AND VISIBILITY

This goes far beyond LinkedIn. Anything you put on LinkedIn should have a professional context to it. Not only that—anything you put on social media should have a professional context. If you wouldn't want your board of directors, CEO or sales manager to see something you're posting, why in the world would you post it? Always maintain a professional visibility across your social applications.

#4. PRETENDING THAT EVERYTHING YOU DO ON LINKEDIN COUNTS AS PROSPECTING

It isn't really prospecting if you're not making actual connections and having actual discussions. The best practice is to send the person an email, leave a message and then send a LinkedIn response that references the other two. You just hit the recipient from three different angles. If there's any interest, you're going to get a response from one of the messages.

#5. SENDING LONG WRITTEN SALES PITCHES VIA INMAIL

InMail messages should be insightful, short and feature a clear call to action. Remember, people could be reading your message on their phone. You should use no more than one or two short paragraphs. It's not a good idea to ask for a first meeting or call in that message. The message should be a brief, customized request to connect with the person on LinkedIn, accompanied by a very concise explanation as to why. For example: You work in the same industry, and you have an interest in something that may add value to him without him having to buy anything. Note: If the person accepts your request to connect, don't immediately fire off an InMail asking for a meeting.

CHAPTER 24

Communicating with CEOs

Reach out the right way, and you gain influence over the buying committee

There are final decision makers on every team. Even if a sales representative wins approval from the rest of the buying committee, sometimes the fate of the project rests solely with the most senior executives. These are the visionaries, the people tasked with making moves that align with top-level business goals and ensuring the most value for their businesses.

CEOs are high-ranking executives who tend to have a unique perspective that should be recognized as you plan your sales strategy. Learn to frame your lead-generation tactics for their specific concerns and you will gain powerful influence over the rest of the buying committee.

THE CEO

Every aspect of the prospect company's business falls under the gaze of its CEO. At a publically traded company, the CEO must answer to a board of directors and multiple stakeholders, stressing the need for both big-picture strategies and metric-level performances.

CEOs oversee the entire organization from profitability to strategic direction and employee relations. They can be directors, decision makers, leaders, managers and executors. They are also becoming more social, frequently posting messages and videos on their company's social network pages.

In a recent study of the new social CEO, Weber Shandwick's Chris Perry noted, "CEOs understand they must be a leading voice with those who follow their company pages, without necessarily amassing and engaging a network of followers on personal social network pages."

In short, CEOs are perhaps the most influential drivers of change within their organizations. They are heavily focused on the business value of any new solution.

THE CEO'S PRIORITIES

CEOs face the challenge of watching the marketplace and making sure their companies remain not only competitive but hold leadership positions. Industry disruption from new technologies and competition can cause CEOs to constantly watch their markets and determine what solutions can counteract disruptions. Answer the following questions to appeal to the CEO and gain interest for your solutions.

What is my solution's value for their business? CEOs think about the big picture, and they evaluate solutions based on the tangible and intangible values for their companies. Financial costs, ROI, technological advancements and process efficiencies are some of the factors that affect business value.

How will my solution improve their bottom line? Demonstrating financial impact is key. Be prepared to show how your solution will either help the company make or save money and when they can expect to see results.

How does my solution impact other areas of their organization? With the weight of the entire company on their shoulders, CEOs are forced to think through the expected and unexpected impacts of any major decision. For example, a step toward automation in one department might have a less than favorable impact on another. Understanding the big picture of the primary and secondary users of your solution will help you paint the bigger picture and overcome any potential hurdles.

Once you understand these major concerns, you can frame your solutions to fit CEO expectations.

COMMUNICATING WITH THE CEO

CEOs will expect you to understand their companies' business objectives and the roles each department plays. Asking basic questions will quickly disqualify your solutions. Instead, try these tactics to speak their language.

Clearly explain the business value. Blinds.com CEO Jay Steinfeld reminds sales professionals that CEOs are people, too. Steinfeld wants sales representatives to ensure he understands "...what's in it for me, besides the undeniable pleasure of doing business with you. Keep the conversation and pitch focused on specific ways you can help me do my job."

Let them do the talking. CEOs are tasked to map their companies' futures, and they are eager to share that vision. Allow them to share their ambitions, concerns and ideas. Listen for the key points that can help you hone your sales strategy and directly address what's important to their business.

Get into their network. Close.io CEO Steli Efti notes the power of referrals, especially for small businesses with limited budgets. Efti states that referrals are "...one of the most important steps to creating a truly scalable sales process. So make it part of your pitch." Eighty-four percent of C-level executives use social media to make their vendor decisions, so include LinkedIn recommendations from previous customers to bolster your case.

CEOs must address immediate business needs while positioning their companies' larger vision for future success. Aligning your solutions and sales techniques to optimize for both can help gain their trust during the sales process.

CHAPTER 25

Lead When You Dance

Use LinkedIn to support your process,
not the prospect's process

Let's say prospective buyer Jane is in a LinkedIn group with you, All About Widgets. You've targeted Jane for a few months, but you've never been able to connect with her. Then Jane reads a nice blog post you wrote, "The Three Most Common Mistakes People Make When Reconditioning Widgets." You shared that blog via your LinkedIn feed, which is how Jane spotted it. She sends you a message via InMail: "Hey, your article was great. We're in the market and looking to select a widget reconditioning vendor this quarter. Your approach looks intriguing. Give me a call." (Actually, Jane is misleading you.

She's sticking with her current vendor, but is looking for another quote from you. She wants to put some competitive pressure onto her present widget reconditioning company.)

You call Jane. You start with a feature dump, basically reciting your brochure. Jane seems attentive enough, though. You have what sounds like a great call. She asks you a lot of questions. You answer them all. (Jane wants to know what you know.)

Then, near the end of the call, Jane shares her product specifications with you and says: "Do me a favor—send me a quote for 1,000." Remembering all that stuff your sales manager told you about securing a spot on the calendar, you ask Jane if you can set up a phone meeting for a week from today to deliver the full presentation.

Jane hedges and commits to nothing. "Just send me the quote. I'll get back to you," she says and hangs up. She later calls you back and thanks you for the quote, says it looks very good and promises to be in touch. Probably within a week or so.

You project the income from this sale on the strength of those two "good calls." Your manager smiles. Then you notice that Jane has entered the sales equivalent of the witness protection program. Weeks pass. You leave messages. You send InMail. You're tempted to send out a search party. Jane has disappeared. Your forecast is shredded. Your manager stops smiling.

Who's in control of the relationship?

Jane is.

No matter how good that conversation sounded to you, it's important for you to avoid falling into the trap of believing that you have something. You have disqualified Jane as a prospect. That's all that happened.

Even though the call was upbeat and enthusiastic from beginning to end, even though Jane reached out to you, even though you're in the same LinkedIn group—nothing happened.

Traditional selling systems would tell you that you did everything you could with Jane. Salespeople schooled in these methods learn to:

- Sell features and benefits.
- Rely heavily on presentation skills to close the deal.
- Employ a broad array of time-tested, manipulative closing techniques.

Here's what they don't tell you. If you follow the traditional selling systems, you will fall into the prospect's system. The prospect will always be leading the dance.

The Sandler Selling System® methodology proposes a very different approach. It challenges salespeople to lead the dance. This is a direct, no-nonsense approach to selling that frames the sales call as a business meeting between equals. In the Sandler system, the salesperson behaves like a highly paid business consultant—and leads the dance.

Here's a brief overview of how it works.

STEP 1: ESTABLISH RAPPORT—STOP ACTING LIKE A SALESPERSON

Prospects erect a defensive wall whenever they think someone is trying to sell them something. That means your first job is to get the prospect comfortable and help him decide, "This person understands problems from my point of view."

STEP 2: ESTABLISH AN UP-FRONT CONTRACT

Before every baseball game, the umpire calls the managers from the two teams together at home plate. The rules of baseball are discussed, including the foul lines, the foul poles, the homerun fence and any unusual circumstances that may apply to that particular ballpark. In sales, the up-front contract serves the same basic purpose. It establishes a clear understanding between the salesperson and the prospect about the conversation's agenda. That's the whole purpose of the up-front contract: to establish a mutually agreeable agenda, so both sides know what they're attempting to accomplish and what each person's role is.

SALES ACCELERATOR

Here are five good ways to set an up-front contract.

1. *On the phone with the person you met via LinkedIn, as you set the appointment*
2. *Via an email invite confirming the appointment (specify action items before meeting)*
3. *At the meeting, before things get started*
4. *At the end of meeting, to confirm what happens next*
5. *Via LinkedIn InMail after the meeting, to confirm in writing what you agreed to verbally*

STEP 3: UNCOVER AND PROBE YOUR PROSPECT'S PAIN

If you do not learn how to uncover the prospect's pain, you will continue to sell using the most difficult of all the antiquated selling principles, the law of averages.

STEP 4: GET ALL THE MONEY ISSUES OUT ON THE TABLE

What is the financial impact of the uncovered issues (pain)? There must be a Budget Step, otherwise there is no certainty you will get paid.

STEP 5: DISCOVER YOUR PROSPECT'S DECISION-MAKING PROCESS

Will the prospect make the decision independently or get help from an associate or spouse? When will the decision be made? Can this prospect make the decision to spend money to fix the pain?

STEP 6: PRESENT A SOLUTION TO ALLEVIATE YOUR PROSPECT'S PAIN

This step is only about showing the prospect how the product or service can get rid of the pain. Nothing more and nothing less.

STEP 7: REINFORCE THE SALE AFTER THE FACT

If you don't have a Post-Sell Step, you may receive a discouraging voicemail from your new "client" saying, "Please call, we need to talk," or an email or text that reads, "Hold up temporarily. I've run into a problem." To avoid that outcome, give the prospect an opportunity to back out while you're still face-to-face—and while you still have a chance to turn the situation around.

Taken together, these seven steps make up the Sandler Submarine.

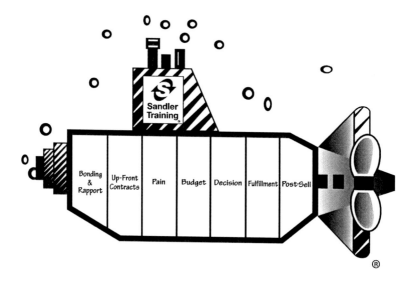

IN A NUTSHELL

One of the most important Sandler strategies for developing a sales opportunity is to qualify stringently and close easily. In fact, as a professional salesperson, you need to be just as diligent about disqualifying people as you are about qualifying them.

Recognize that there are people for whom what you have to offer is either not appropriate or is outside of their ability to take advantage. You may run into people who want what you have, but are not willing and able to do what needs to be done to get it. You want to uncover their true status as early as possible and spend as little of your precious time with these people as you can.

Of course, there are also those who definitely need what you have and have the wherewithal and desire to get it from you. Obviously you want to be spending as much of your time with these people as you possibly can. You want to be laser-focused with them about all the reasons to take action now, as opposed to putting off action.

When we talk about "qualifying" a prospect, we don't mean just making sure the person has a pulse and is willing to speak. To qualify in the sense we mean, you have to be willing to talk with the prospect as a peer about the pain he is experiencing, about the budget available to remove that pain and about the decision process around allocating that budget. You have to decide, together, that it makes sense to move forward.

Look closely at the results of the traditional sales process, and then compare it with the results of the Sandler sales process. You will soon see the advantage of politely disengaging from, and declining to create quotes for, people like Jane—unless and until she's willing to dance your way.

EPILOGUE

Success with the Sandler Selling System methodology depends on the development of relationships based on integrity—and so does a successful approach to professional selling using LinkedIn. In this book, we've tried to build integrity into both the learning and the selling processes, and we'd like to think that what we've shared has been helpful. We look forward to helping you continue your journey towards success, however you define it.

Stay in touch. Please visit us at www.sandler.com!

SANDLER ENTERPRISE SELLING

Enterprise sales are typically those featuring multiple decision makers and influencers, longer sales cycles and the coordination of multiple work groups on both the buying side and the selling side. There are six stages to the Sandler Enterprise Selling (SES) program, which incorporates all the principles of the familiar Sandler Submarine.

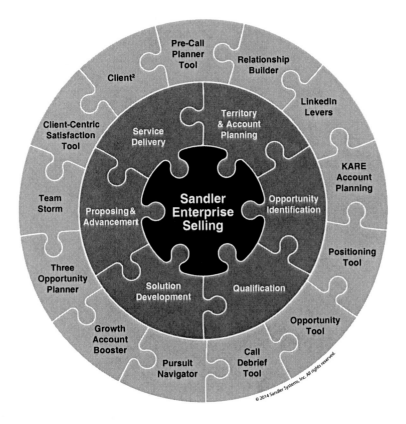

For more information on the SES program, call 410-559-2003 or visit www.sandler.com/enterpriseselling.

Let's connect on LinkedIn!

bit.ly/ses_linkedin

This link will take you to LinkedIn's
Sandler Enterprise Selling Group.
Join the discussion!

CONGRATULATIONS!

LinkedIn the Sandler Way
includes a complimentary seminar!

Take this opportunity to personally experience the non-traditional sales training and reinforcement coaching that has been recognized internationally for decades.

Companies in the Fortune 1000 as well as thousands of small- to medium-sized businesses choose Sandler for sales, leadership, management, and a wealth of other skill-building programs. Now, it's your turn, and it's free!

You'll learn the latest practical, tactical, feet-in-the-street sales methods directly from your neighborhood Sandler trainers! They're knowledgeable, friendly, and informed about your local selling environment.

Here's how you redeem YOUR FREE SEMINAR invitation.

1. Go to www.Sandler.com and click on Find Training Location (top blue bar).
2. Select your location.
3. Review the list of all the Sandler trainers in your area.
4. Call your local Sandler trainer, mention *LinkedIn the Sandler Way*, and reserve your place at the next seminar!